Shark Attack!

By Joy Cowley

Illustrated by Mike Lacey

DOMINIE PRESS

Pearson Learning Group

Paperback ISBN 0-7685-1077-5
Printed in Singapore
    7 8   09 08 07

Dominie
Press
Pearson Learning Group

1-800-321-3106
www.pearsonlearning.com

Table of Contents

Chapter One

It's Too Cold!

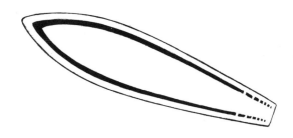

Jack woke up before dawn.
The storm was over,
but the surf was still high.
He could hear the growl
of waves on the beach.
He banged on Emilio's door.
"Wake up, Sunshine!"
he called to his friend.

"Grab your wet suit.
We're out of here!"

Emilio gave a sleepy groan
and said, "It's too cold!"

Jack opened the door.
He picked up Emilio's fins
and threw them onto his bed.
"Don't be such a wimp!
Come on, hit the deck
while I make the coffee."

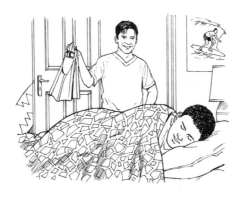

"It's still dark!" Emilio complained.

Jack laughed.
"It won't be by the time
we get down to the beach.
Surfing at sunrise!
Man, you can't beat it!"

Chapter Two

A Surfing Nut

Emilio liked to ride the waves,
but he wasn't a surfing nut
like his friend Jack.
Jack would surf all day
and all night, if he could.

Emilio hated cold, cold water.

He dragged his board
across the wet sand.
There was a lot of seaweed
and driftwood on the beach,
and the water was still brown
from the storm.
The waves were huge.
They rose like muddy walls
and crashed into dirty foam.

Emilio yawned.

No, he definitely didn't want
to surf this morning.
But Jack was like the weather,
there was no stopping him,
and they always had this rule—
no one rode the waves alone.
So Emilio was going to surf
whether he liked it or not.

At least it was going to be
a good day. The sky was clear.
The first rays of the sun
were warming the air.

The water, though, was very cold.
It was all right for Jack.
He was wearing a winter wet suit.
Emilio's suit was summer weight.
His bones would turn to ice.

Chapter Three

Under the Water

Jack knew this beach
like the back of his hand.
He knew the tides, the currents,
and the way the sea behaved.
He understood the movement
of water under his board,
the pull that said, *Yes! Now!*
or, *No! Wait!*

11

He looked at Emilio,

who was paddling near the shore.

Emilio had been his best friend
since their kindergarten days,
but Emilio didn't share
Jack's love of surfing.

Jack secretly thought
that Emilio was a pussycat
when it came to real adventure.

He waved at Emilio
to come out deeper,
and he watched as his friend
paddled toward him.

He was waiting and watching
when the thing hit him.

Crunch!

The blow was so strong,
he thought that a boat
had run into him.
His board went one way
and he went another.

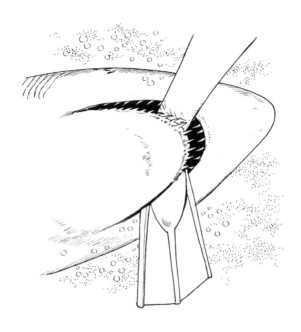

He went under the water
and thrashed around,
trying to get air.
Then he was hit again,
this time in the leg.
He realized what it was.

A shark!

Chapter Four
Hold On!

Emilio saw it happen.
Jack had been sitting on his board.
Then, suddenly, the board flew up.
Jack went under, and the sea
looked as though it was boiling.
In the middle of it all,
a dark fin appeared.
Jack was being attacked
by a shark.

There was no way of knowing
how many sharks were out there.
Emilio tried not to think
about that. He paddled fast.

"Hold on, Jack! Hold on!"
he called, although he knew
that his friend couldn't hear him.

He saw Jack's head and arm.
He saw the shark's tail.
What if the shark was big enough
to pull Jack under?

He paddled faster,
his arms aching
and his breath hurting his chest.

"Hold on, Jack! I'm coming!"

Chapter Five

Something Grabbed His Hand

Jack was fighting for breath.
The shark had his right ankle.
He felt no pain,
but his leg was trapped,
and he knew he would drown
if he couldn't get free.

Jack gulped water and choked.
His head came above the surface,
then he was under again.

Don't panic! Don't panic!
he tried to tell himself.

The shark was twisting,
its jaws firmly around his ankle.
Jack spun around in the water
with the shark.

He felt its cold, rough skin.
He tried to hit it.
It would not let go.
Jack knew that he was
going to die.

He waved his arms around,
trying to reach the surface.
He saw a dark shape.
Then something
grabbed his hand.
Another shark! he thought.
But no, it was Emilio
on his surfboard.

Emilio dragged him up,
coughing and gasping.

"Shark!" Jack tried to say.

Emilio held on to him.
"I can see it," he replied.

Chapter Six

Six Feet Long

Emilio lay on his board,
holding Jack's hands.
As a wave lifted them,
he saw the shark clearly.
It was about six feet long
and it had a long tail.
Its mouth was around
Jack's wet suit and dive boot.
There was a dark brown stain
in the muddy water.

Emilio pulled Jack's arms
across the board.
"Hold on!" he cried.
"Don't let go!"
Then he jumped in
on top of the shark.

He didn't know
what he was going to do.
He wrapped his arms and legs
around the shark
and tried to hold on.
The dorsal fin twisted
against his wet suit.
He went under the water,
his arms still around
the shark's fins.
He saw the shark's eye
close to his face.

Still holding on,
Emilio put his thumbs
against the shark's eyes.

The shark opened its jaws
and let Jack's leg go.

It swam away.

Chapter Seven

Wrapped in Bandages

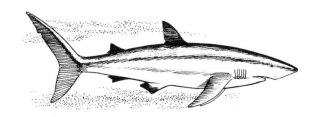

Jack knew he had been lucky.
Because the morning
had been cold,
he'd worn his winter wet suit
and his dive boots inside his fins.
They had protected his leg.
But it was his friend Emilio
who had saved his life.

On the hospital bed,
Jack showed Emilio his ankle
wrapped in bandages.
"I've got twenty-two stitches,"
he said, "but no broken bones."

"I found your board," Emilio said.
"It had a huge bite out of it."

"Wow!" said Jack.
"That could have been me!"

"It nearly was you,"
Emilio reminded him.

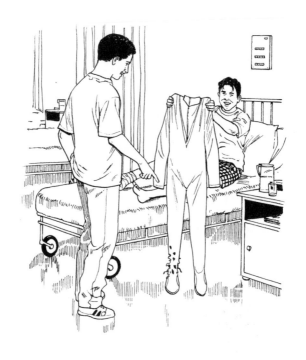

Jack grinned at his friend.

"Hey, man!" he said.

"If I ever call you a wimp again,
you can have my winter wet suit."

Emilio laughed. "It's no good!"
he said. "It's got holes in it."